Re
1
b
te

colourful
container
gardens

colourful
container
gardens

Vibrant schemes for pots and planters

Stephanie Donaldson

southwater

This edition is published by Southwater, an imprint of Anness Publishing Ltd,
Hermes House, 88–89 Blackfriars Road, London SE1 8HA;
tel. 020 7401 2077; fax 020 7633 9499

www.southwaterbooks.com; www.annesspublishing.com

If you like the images in this book and would like to investigate using them
for publishing, promotions or advertising, please visit our website
www.practicalpictures.com for more information.

UK agent: The Manning Partnership Ltd;
tel. 01225 478444; fax 01225 478440;
sales@manning-partnership.co.uk
UK distributor: Grantham Book Services Ltd;
tel. 01476 541080; fax 01476 541061; orders@gbs.tbs-ltd.co.uk
North American agent/distributor: National Book Network;
tel. 301 459 3366; fax 301 429 5746; www.nbnbooks.com
Australian agent/distributor: Pan Macmillan Australia;
tel. 1300 135 113; fax 1300 135 103; customer.service@macmillan.com.au
New Zealand agent/distributor: David Bateman Ltd;
tel. (09) 415 7664; fax (09) 415 8892

Publisher Joanna Lorenz
Managing Editor Judith Simons
Project Editor Mariano Kälfors
Designers Janet James & Jane Coney
Photography Marie O'Hara
Production Controller Don Campaniello

ETHICAL TRADING POLICY

Because of our ongoing ecological investment programme, you, as our customer,
can have the pleasure and reassurance of knowing that a tree is
being cultivated on your behalf to naturally replace the materials used to
make the book you are holding. For further information about this
scheme, go to www.annesspublishing.com/trees

PUBLISHER'S NOTE

Although the advice and information in this book are believed to be
accurate and true at the time of going to press, neither the authors nor
the publisher can accept any legal responsibility or liability for any
errors or omissions that may be made.

PAGE 1: *An old spraypainted loom chair amidst foliage
provides an eyecatching setting for a lone container.*

PAGE 2 AND 3: *A splash of hot colours in witty
containers vie and clash in a vibrant display.*

RIGHT: *A cluster of evergreens augmented for the festive season
by a potted topiary tree of blue spruce and fir cones.*

OPPOSITE: *Ornamental cabbage!*

Contents

Introduction

Whether you have a large country garden, a tiny courtyard or simply a balcony or windowsill, containers add an extra dimension to the effects you can create. To begin with, there is a wonderful range of inspiring containers to chose from, so you are sure to find something that will harmonize with the surroundings – rustic and quaint, formal and elegant, or the latest in chic design.

ABOVE: *Topiary ivy with white petunias. Plant the ivy ahead to allow it time to establish an outline.*

ABOVE: *A group of spring flowers provide a charming display on a windowsill.*

OPPOSITE: *An old wicker mannequin makes an amusing and unexpected frame for topiary ivy.*

RIGHT: *Here a windowbox is used to stunning effect with a colour-coordinated display of bedding plants.*

Temporary container plantings makes it easy to change colour schemes with each season. You can also create containers with a framework of permanent plants, and then add bedding plants, changing these every year.

Enjoy the pleasure of creating your own colour combinations.

Getting Started

Before you begin planting, take some time to explore the range of possible containers – as well as those available commercially you may find items that you can recycle or transform into something interesting and unusual.

You then need to consider the type of plants that you can grow. Many are tolerant of both sunny and shady conditions, but there are some that will only do well in a sunny spot, while others will grow very happily in shade.

The following pages will help you to design, plant and care for a whole range of containers and bring ever-changing colour to your home.

Colour-theme plantings

Create impact in the garden by colour-theming seasonal plantings to tune in with their surroundings. This works best with plants in containers as the containers can be chosen to tone and blend with the walls, then planted with flowers in complementary colours. Once the blooms are over, they can be replaced by new plantings for the next season. You do not always have to match the colours; you may decide to use contrasting colours instead. In this way, the garden looks fresh and bright all year round and you have several scene changes to enjoy as the seasons pass.

ABOVE: *The blue-green and purple tones of ornamental cabbage look fabulous in a galvanized grey bucket, set against the blue-green of a painted fence.*

OPPOSITE: *An orange-yellow poppy and cream-coloured violas look stunning planted in beige pots, set against the warm ochre shades of a brick wall.*

ABOVE: *This pot has been painted in stripes to link the green background and pink blooms of a wonderful hebe.*

Colour-splash plantings

Just as you can decorate the inside of your home with colourful flower arrangements, so you can do the same outside. Use pots of flowering plants to provide a colourful splash in a prominent part of the garden or to decorate the outdoor living area when entertaining. Create an immediate colour impact by choosing a colour theme and teaming containers and plants in toning shades. Try painting some terracotta pots specially to match your favourite flowers. You could also make a tablescape for a special occasion, using a variety of containers and seasonal flowering plants in hot clashing colours or in cool shades of blue, purple and white.

ABOVE: *Simple and magical, it is as though the rich colouring of the tulips has leaked out of the petals and dripped down the side of the pots.*

ABOVE: *Even a couple of ordinary terracotta garden pots hanging on the wall make interesting decorative detail, especially when they are both planted with a froth of white blooms.*

LEFT: *The variegated foliage of 'Tom West', here underplanted with ivy, develops a rich pink colouring when grown in a sunny position.*

ABOVE: *Bright, bold, hothouse colours are very effective in groups.*
Try to find equally brightly coloured planters and containers.

The best plants for containers

Annuals and Biennials

Whether you raise them yourself from seed in the greenhouse or on the kitchen window-sill, or buy them in strips from the garden centre for an instant effect, fast-growing annuals and biennials will quickly and cheaply fill baskets and boxes and flower prolifically all summer to produce eye-catching effects. Choose compact varieties that will not need support. Trailing annuals such as lobelia, nasturtiums and dwarf sweet peas are all invaluable for hanging baskets. Some perennial species, including petunias, pelargoniums and busy Lizzies (impatiens), are normally grown as annuals.

Tender Perennials

Beautiful tender and half-hardy plants such as osteospermums, verbenas, pelargoniums, petunias and fuchsias are ideal for containers, where their showy flowers can be fully appreciated. Raise new plants from cuttings for next season. If you buy young, tender plants from the garden centre in the spring, don't be tempted to put newly planted boxes or baskets outside until all danger of frost is past.

ABOVE: *Trailing nasturtiums make a glorious display, providing colour from early summer.*

LEFT: *Petunias and pelargoniums are tender perennials, which are often grown as annuals.*

BELOW: *Containers of spring bulbs such as these yellow tulips cannot fail to delight.*

Evergreen Perennials

Evergreen non-woody perennials such as ajugas, bergenias and *Carex oshimensis* 'Evergold' are always useful for providing colour and foliage in the winter, but look best as part of a mixed planting.

For single plantings, try *Agapanthus africanus* or *A. orientalis* with their blue flowers on tall stems. For a more architectural shape, consider one of the many different eryngiums (sea holly). *E. agavifolium* is particularly attractive, and has greenish-white flowers in late summer.

Border Perennials

Few people bother to grow perennials in containers, but if you have a paved garden, or would like to introduce them to the patio, don't be afraid to experiment. Dicentras, agapanthus, and many ornamental grasses are among the plants that you might want to try, but there are very many more that you should be able to succeed with – and they will cost you nothing if you divide a plant already in the border.

Bulbs

Bulbs, particularly the spring varieties make ideal container plants. Bulbs should be planted at twice the depth of their own length. They can be packed in as tight as you like, and even in layers, so that you get a repeat-showing after the first display. Note that when planting lilies (the white, scented, fail-safe *Lilium regale* is a fine choice if you have never tried them before), they need excellent drainage, so put in an extra layer of grit at the bottom. And to prevent spearing the bulb later on with a plant support, insert this in the compost at the same time.

Shrubs for Tubs

Camellias are perfect shrubs for tubs, combining attractive, glossy evergreen foliage with beautiful spring flowers. *Camellia* x *williamsii* and *C. japonica* hybrids are a good choice. Many rhododendrons and azaleas are also a practical proposition, and if you have a chalky (alkaline) soil this is the best way to grow these plants – provided you fill the container with an ericaceous compost (soil mix).

Many hebes make good container plants (but not for very cold or exposed areas), and there are many attractively variegated varieties. The yellow-leaved *Choisya ternata* 'Sundance' and variegated yuccas such as *Yucca filamentosa* 'Variegata' and *Y. gloriosa* 'Variegata' are also striking shrubs for containers.

For some winter interest, try *Viburnum tinus*.

Topiary for Pots

Topiarized box is ideal for a pot. However, it is relatively slow growing at about 30cm (12in) a year. It may be best to buy a mature, ready-shaped plant, although you miss the fun of doing the pruning.

ABOVE: *If your garden cannot support lime-hating rhododendrons, do not despair. They can easily be grown in pots, in ericaceous compost (soil mix), and will flower happily for years.*

LEFT: *Pots on plinths and fruit trees in tubs create a marvellous architectural effect, with plenty of striking verticals.*

Trees for Tubs

In a small garden, planting small trees in containers can work well. The restricted root-run usually keeps them compact and they never reach the proportions of trees planted in the ground. Even in a small garden, some height is useful.

Choose trees that are naturally small if possible. Laburnums, crab apples (and some of the upright-growing and compact eating apples on dwarfing root-stocks), *Prunus* 'Amanogawa' (a flowering cherry with narrow, upright growth), and even trees as potentially large as *Acer platanoides* 'Drummondii' (a variegated maple) will be happy in a large pot or tub for a number of years. Small weeping trees also look good. Try *Salix caprea pendula* or *Cotoneaster* 'Hybridus Pendulus' (which has cascades of red berries in autumn). Even the pretty dome-shaped, grey-leaved *Pyrus salicifolia* 'Pendula' is a possibility.

These must have a heavy pot with a minimum inside diameter of 38cm (15in), and a loam-based compost (soil mix). Even then they are liable to blow over in very strong winds unless you pack some other hefty pots around them during stormy weather.

Fiery Reds, Oranges & Yellows

Fiery reds and brilliant yellows reflect the heat and brightness of summer and make for an exciting mix of carnival colours. Try bringing a little touch of the exotic to your garden by planting vivid red pelargoniums in brightly painted pots. Fire and earth will be reflected in terracotta containers of scarlet fuchsia and orange nasturtiums, and vibrant yellows, oranges and reds will glow in a sunny wall basket.

As the season progresses, deep bronze and golds will reflect the trees in the park and the leaves in the streets and usher in the autumn.

Dark drama

The intense purple of the heliotrope usually dominates other plants, but here it is teamed with a selection of equally dramatic colours – *Dahlia* 'Bednall Beauty', with its purple foliage and dark red flowers, black grass and red and purple verbenas – to make a stunning display.

MATERIALS

60cm (24in) terracotta
  windowbox
Polystyrene (plastic foam) or
  other suitable drainage material
Compost (soil mix)
Slow-release plant food granules

PLANTS

Heliotrope
2 Dahlia 'Bednall Beauty'
Black grass (Ophiopogon
  planiscapus *'Nigrescens')*
2 purple trailing verbenas
2 red trailing verbenas

BLACK GRASS

VERBENAS

DAHLIA

HELIOTROPE

1 Fill the bottom of the windowbox with broken polystyrene (plastic foam) or other suitable drainage material.

2 Fill the windowbox with compost (soil mix), adding in 3 teaspoons of slow-release plant food granules. Plant the heliotrope centrally at the back of the windowbox, gently teasing apart the roots, if necessary.

3 Plant the dahlias in the back corners of the windowbox.

4 Plant the black grass in front of the heliotrope.

5 Plant the purple verbenas at the back between the heliotrope and the dahlias.

6 Plant the red verbenas at the front in either corner. This is a large container so it is best to position it before watering. Put it where it will benefit from full sun, then water thoroughly.

GARDENER'S TIP

Dahlias can be overwintered by digging up the tubers after the first frosts, cutting the stems back to 15cm (6in) and drying them off before storing in slightly damp peat in a frost-free shed. Start into growth again in spring and plant out after all danger of frost is past.

PLANT IN LATE SPRING OR EARLY SUMMER

Flame-red flowers in terracotta

The intense red flowers of the pelargoniums, verbena and nasturtiums are emphasized by a few yellow nasturtiums and the variegated ivy, but cooled slightly by the soothing blue-green of the nasturtium's umbrella-shaped leaves.

NASTURTIUM

VERBENA

IVY

PELARGONIUM

MATERIALS

50cm (20in) terracotta window box
Crocks (broken pots) or other suitable drainage material
Compost (soil mix)
Slow-release plant food granules

PLANTS

2 red zonal pelargoniums
2 nasturtiums – 1 red, 1 yellow
Red verbena
2 variegated ivies

1 Place a layer of crocks (broken pots) or other suitable drainage material in the base of the windowbox.

2 Fill the container with compost (soil mix), adding 3 teaspoons of slow-release plant food granules.

3 Plant the pelargoniums either side of the centre of the windowbox.

4 Plant a nasturtium at each end of the windowbox, in the back corners.

5 Plant the verbena in the centre of the windowbox.

6 Plant the ivies in front of the nasturtiums in the corners. Water well, leave to drain, and place in a sunny position.

GARDENER'S TIP

Nasturtiums are prone to attack by blackfly. Treat at the first sign of infestation with a suitable insecticide and the plants will remain healthy.

PLANT IN LATE SPRING OR EARLY SUMMER

Good enough to eat

All the plants in this basket bear an edible crop: the tomato fruit, nasturtium flowers and parsley leaves. You could even impress your family or guests with a 'hanging basket salad', using all three together.

MATERIALS

36cm (14in) hanging basket
Sphagnum moss
Compost (soil mix)
Slow-release plant food granules

PLANTS

6 parsley plants
3 trailing nasturtiums
3 'Tumbler' tomatoes, or similar

PARSLEY

TRAILING NASTURTIUM

TOMATO

GARDENER'S TIP

If you would prefer to grow your plants organically, plant this basket using an organic compost (soil mix) and use natural plant foods such as pelleted chicken manure or a liquid seaweed feed.

PLANT IN LATE SPRING OR EARLY SUMMER

1 Line the lower half of the basket with moss.

2 Plant three parsley plants into the side of the basket by resting the root-balls on the moss, and feeding the leaves through the side of the basket.

3 Line the basket to just below the rim and fill with compost (soil mix). Work a teaspoon of plant food granules into the top of the compost. Plant three nasturtium plants into the side of the basket, just below the rim.

4 Finish lining the basket with moss, being careful to tuck plenty of moss around the nasturtiums.

5 Plant the tomato plants in the top of the basket.

6 Plant the remaining three parsley plants amongst the tomatoes in the top of the basket. Water well and hang in a sunny position. Liquid feed regularly.

Bronze and gold winners

Bronze pansies and mimulus and golden green lysimachias take the medals in this striking arrangement, with richly coloured heuchera adding to the unusual mixture of tones. This arrangement will work most successfully in a partially shaded situation.

MATERIALS

40cm (16in) hanging basket
Sphagnum moss
Compost (soil mix)
Slow-release plant food granules

PLANTS

Heuchera 'Bressingham Bronze'
3 bronze-coloured pansies (viola)
3 bronze-coloured mimulus
3 Lysimachia nummularia 'Aurea'

LYSIMACHIA

MIMULUS

PANSY

HEUCHERA

1 Line the basket with moss.

2 Fill the basket with compost (soil mix), working a teaspoon of plant food granules into the top layer of compost.

3 Plant the heuchera in the middle of the basket.

4 Plant the pansies, evenly spaced around the heuchera.

5 Plant the three mimulus between the pansies.

6 Plant the lysimachias around the edge of the basket. Water well and hang in light shade.

GARDENER'S TIP

At the end of the season the heuchera can be planted in the border or in another container. It will do best in partial shade, as full sun tends to scorch and discolour the leaves.

PLANT IN SPRING

Vibrant reds and sunny yellows

This basket is an exciting mix of glowing colours and contrasting leaf shapes. A bright red verbena and the pineapple-scented salvia tumble from the basket, intertwined with red and yellow nasturtiums and a striking golden grass.

MATERIALS

36cm (14in) hanging basket
Sphagnum moss
Compost (soil mix)
Slow-release plant food granules

PLANTS

4 trailing nasturtiums
Golden grass Hakonechloa *'Alboaurea', or similar*
Salvia elegans
Verbena *'Lawrence Johnston'*

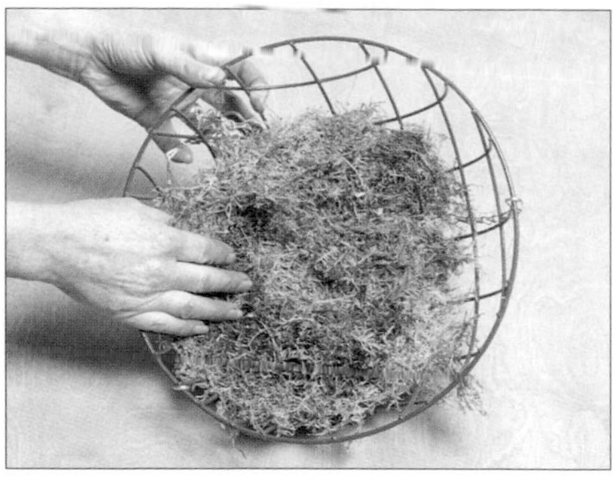

1 Line the bottom half of the basket with moss.

2 Plant three of the nasturtiums into the side of the basket by resting the root-balls on the moss, and carefully feeding the leaves through the basket.

3 Line the rest of the basket with moss and fill with compost (soil mix). Work a teaspoon of plant food granules into the compost. Plant the golden grass to one side of the basket.

4 Plant the salvia a third of the way round the edge of the basket from the grass.

5 Plant the verbena at an equal distance from the salvia and the golden grass.

6 Plant the remaining nasturtium in the centre. Water well and hang in a sunny position.

GARDENER'S TIP

Nasturtiums are wonderful plants for hanging baskets – vigorous, colourful and undemanding – but they can be disfigured by blackfly. Spray at the first sign of an infestation with an insecticide which will not harm beneficial insects.

PLANT IN LATE SPRING OR EARLY SUMMER

Summer carnival

The orange markings on the throats of some of the mimulus flowers look wonderful with the orange-flowered pelargonium in this colourful basket. By the end of the season, trails of lysimachia leaves will form a waterfall of foliage around the base.

MATERIALS

36cm (14in) basket
Sphagnum moss
Compost (soil mix)
Slow-release plant food granules

PLANTS

Orange-flowered zonal
*   pelargonium*
3 Lysimachia nummularia 'Aurea'
3 mimulus

LYSIMACHIA

MIMULUS

PELARGONIUM

GARDENER'S TIP

Dead-head the flowers regularly to encourage repeat flowering, and if the mimulus start to get leggy, cut back the offending stems to a leaf joint. New shoots will soon appear.

PLANT IN LATE SPRING OR EARLY SUMMER

1 Line the basket with moss and fill it with compost (soil mix), working a teaspoon of slow-release plant food granules into the top layer. Plant the pelargonium in the centre of the basket.

2 Plant the lysimachia, evenly spaced, around the edge of the basket, angling the plants so they will trail over the sides.

3 Plant the mimulus between the lysimachia. Water the hanging basket thoroughly and hang in a sunny spot.

A floral chandelier

MATERIALS

36cm (14in) hanging basket
Sphagnum moss
Compost (soil mix)
Slow-release plant food granules

PLANTS

3 yellow lantanas, 2 variegated,
*   1 green-leaved*
2 Bidens ferulifolia
5 African marigolds (tagetes)

AFRICAN
MARIGOLDS

LANTANA

BIDENS

The chandelier shape is a result of combining the spreading bidens with upright lantanas and marigolds. Since the variegated-leaf lantanas proved very slow to establish, a more vigorous green-leaved form was added later. As the season progresses, the strongly marked leaves of the variegated plants will become more dominant.

1 Line the basket with moss. Fill it with compost (soil mix), working a teaspoon of plant food granules into the top layer. Plant the lantana in the centre.

2 Plant the two bidens opposite one another at the edge of the basket.

3 Plant the African marigolds around the lantana plants. Water thoroughly and hang in a sunny position.

GARDENER'S TIP

To complete the chandelier, make candle holders by twisting thick garden wire around the base of yellow candles and add them to the hanging basket.

PLANT IN LATE SPRING OR EARLY SUMMER

Gentle Pinks, Purples & Blues

*T*oning shades of blue, a medley of pinks and gentle lavender complemented by soft silvers, cream and white create a cool and flowing atmosphere. Different shades of pink petunias and verbenas combined with white alyssum make a charming wall basket, while the delicate silvery filigree foliage of senecio, together with the deep purple leaves of a heuchera, softens a lavender-themed planting in a white-painted windowbox. Underplanting with trailing plants ensures that flowers cascade down the side of baskets.

An instant garden

There is not always time to wait for a windowbox to grow and this is one solution. Fill a container with potted plants and, as the season progresses, you can ring the changes by removing those that are past their best and introducing new plants.

HELICHRYSUM

PETUNIA

CONVOLVULUS

LAVENDER

VIOLA

BACOPA

MATERIALS

64cm (25in) galvanized tin
*   windowbox*
Clay granules
5 1-litre (5in) plastic pots
Compost (soil mix)

PLANTS

Lavender (Lavandula pinnata)
2 blue petunias
Convolvulus sabatius
Blue bacopa
Helichrysum petiolare
Viola *'Jupiter'*

GARDENER'S TIP

When using a container without drainage holes, take care not to overwater or the roots will become waterlogged.
Check after heavy rain, too, and empty away any excess water.

PLANT IN LATE SPRING OR EARLY SUMMER

1 Fill the base of the container with clay granules or similar drainage material.

2 Pot up the lavender into one of the pots.

3 Pot up one of the petunias with the convolvulus.

4 Pot up the other petunia with the bacopa.

5 Pot up the helichrysum.

6 Pot up the viola and arrange the pots in the windowbox.

Sapphires for spring

Deep blue pansies are surrounded by gentian-blue anagallis and underplanted with golden helichrysums in this richly coloured basket.

MATERIALS

30cm (12in) hanging basket
Sphagnum moss
Compost (soil mix)
Slow-release plant food granules

PLANTS

3 Helichrysum petiolare 'Aureum'
3 deep blue pansies
3 blue anagallis

ANAGALLIS

HELICHRYSUM

PANSY

1 Line the lower half of the basket with moss before planting the helichrysums in the sides of the basket.

2 Rest the root-balls on the moss, and carefully guide the foliage through the wires.

3 Line the rest of the basket with moss and fill with compost (soil mix), working a teaspoon of plant food into the top layer. Plant the pansies, evenly spaced, in the top of the basket.

4 Plant the anagallis between the pansies. Water the basket thoroughly and hang in partial sun.

GARDENER'S TIP

The golden-green colour of *Helichrysum petiolare* 'Aureum' is far stronger if the plants are not in full sun. Too much sun tends to fade the colouring.

PLANT IN SPRING

Scented windowbox

The soft silvers and blues of the flowers and foliage beautifully complement this verdigris windowbox. The scent of the lavender and petunias will drift magically through open windows.

MATERIALS

60cm (24in) windowbox
Gravel or similar drainage material
Equal mix loam-based compost (soil mix) and container compost
Slow-release plant food granules

PLANTS

2 lavenders
2 pale blue petunias
4 deep blue petunias
4 Chaenorhinum glareosum (or lilac lobelia)
6 Helichrysum petiolare

PETUNIA

CHAENORHINUM

LAVENDER

HELICHRYSUM

GARDENER'S TIP

To keep a densely planted container like this looking its best it is necessary to feed regularly with a liquid feed, or more simply to mix slow-release plant food granules into the surface of the compost (soil mix) to last the whole summer. Cut back the lavender heads after flowering to ensure bushy flowering plants again next year.

PLANT IN LATE SPRING OR EARLY SUMMER

1 Fill the bottom 5cm (2in) of the windowbox with drainage material and half-fill with compost (soil mix). Position the lavender plants, loosening the soil around the roots before planting, as they will establish better this way.

2 Now arrange the flowering plants around the lavender, leaving spaces for the helichrysums between them.

3 Finally, add the helichrysums and fill between the plants with compost (soil mix), pressing firmly so that no air gaps are left around the roots. Place in a sunny position and water regularly.

Filigree foliage

The purply-black leaves of this heuchera are all the more stunning when surrounded by the delicate silver-and-green filigree foliage of senecio, the tender *Lavandula pinnata* and the soft lilac-coloured flowers of the bacopa and the brachycome daisies. The plants are grown in a white plastic planter which is concealed inside an elegant wooden windowbox.

MATERIALS

76cm (30in) plastic windowbox
Compost (soil mix)
Slow-release plant food granules
90cm (3ft) wooden windowbox
  (optional)

PLANTS

Heuchera *'Palace Purple'*
2 lavenders
2 blue brachycome daisies
3 Senecio cineraria 'Silver Dust'
2 blue bacopa

SENECIO

LAVENDER

BRACHYCOME

BACOPA

HEUCHERA

1 Check drainage holes are open in the base of the planter and, if not, drill or punch them out. Fill the windowbox with compost (soil mix), mixing in 2 teaspoons of plant food granules. Plant the heuchera in the centre.

2 Plant the two lavenders on either side of the heuchera.

3 Plant the two brachycome daisies at each end of the windowbox.

4 Place the three senecios at the front of the box between the brachycomes.

5 Plant the two bacopa between the senecio and the heuchera.

6 Water thoroughly and lift into place in the wooden window-box, if using. Place in full or partial sun.

GARDENER'S TIP

Wooden windowboxes can be assembled so they are self-watering where access is difficult for daily watering. A variety of self-watering containers are available and come with full instructions for their use.

PLANT IN SPRING

Blooming old boots

This is a blooming wonderful way to recycle an old pair of boots, the bigger the better. It just goes to show that almost anything can be used to grow plants in, as long as it has a few holes in the bottom for drainage. Try an old football, a sports bag, or even an old hat for plant containers with lots of character.

MATERIALS

Knife
Old pair of working boots
Compost (soil mix)

PLANTS

Selection of bedding plants such as impatiens, pelargoniums, verbenas, pansies and lobelias

BEDDING PLANTS

1 Using a knife very carefully, make some holes in between the stitching of the sole for drainage. It helps if there are holes there already.

2 Fill the boots with compost (soil mix), pushing it right down so there are no air spaces.

3 Plant flowers like pelargoniums, that can cope with hot dry places, and verbenas which will trail over the edge.

4 Squeeze in a pansy with a contrasting flower colour and a trailing lobelia plant. Lobelia grows in the smallest of spaces and will delicately tumble over the edge.

5 The boots need watering every day in the summer, and bloom even better if some plant food is mixed into the water once a week.

PLANT IN SPRING

Standard fuchsia

Fuchsia 'Tom West' is an excellent hardy variety which was raised in 1853. Here, underplanted with variegated ivy, and benefiting from the large Chinese-style glazed pot, the display has a very modern chic appeal.

MATERIALS

Large glazed pot, at least 70cm
  (28in) diameter
Crocks (broken pots)
Peat-free compost (soil mix)
Slow-release plant food granules

PLANTS

1 half-standard Fuchsia 'Tom
  West'
6 variegated ivies

FUCHSIA

IVY

1 Cover the drainage hole in the base of the pot with the crocks (broken pots). This prevents it from becoming blocked and facilitates the free drainage of excess water.

2 Almost fill the pot with peat-free compost (soil mix). Add slow-release plant food granules to the compost.

3 Remove the half-standard fuchsia from its pot, and lower it gently on to the compost so that the top of its root-ball is slightly lower than the lip of the pot.

4 Add more compost (soil mix). Plant the variegated ivies around the base of the fuchsia. Fill in the gaps between the root-balls, and tease the ivies' stems and foliage across the compost surface. Water to settle the compost.

GARDENER'S TIP

The variegated foliage of 'Tom West' develops a lovely rich pink colouring when grown in a sunny position. The best foliage colour is on the young growth, so regular pinching out of new stem tips will ensure a colourful plant.

PLANT IN EARLY SPRING OR EARLY SUMMER

Neutral Whites & Greens

Planting schemes with only white flowers can be surprisingly effective. Without the distraction of other colours you can see a whole range of subtle variations in the shades of white combined with the many different greens of the foliage.

The soft, seductive scent of a star-jasmine in a container beside a door will be enjoyed by all who pass through; a silver and white wall basket looks good against a weathered background; and an impressive all-white windowbox is an ideal wedding display.

White flowers and painted terracotta

There are plenty of inexpensive windowboxes available, but they do tend to look rather similar. Why not customize a bought windowbox to give it a touch of individuality? This deep blue painted windowbox creates an interesting setting for the cool white pelargonium and verbenas.

MATERIALS

45cm (18in) terracotta
*   windowbox painted blue*
Crocks (broken pots) or other
*   suitable drainage material*
Compost (soil mix)
Slow-release plant food granules

PLANTS

White pelargonium
2 variegated felicias
2 white trailing verbenas

FELICIA

VERBENA

PELARGONIUM

1 Cover the base of the window box with a layer of crocks (broken pots) or similar drainage material.

2 Fill the windowbox with compost (soil mix). Add 2 teaspoons of slow-release plant food granules. Plant the pelargonium in the centre of the windowbox.

3 Plant a felicia on either side of the pelargonium at the back of the container. Plant a verbena on either side of the pelargonium at the front of the windowbox. Water well and stand in a sunny position.

GARDENER'S TIP

White pelargoniums need regular dead-heading to look their best. Old flowerheads discolour and quickly spoil the appearance of the plant.

PLANT IN LATE SPRING OR EARLY SUMMER

Topiary ivy with white petunias

Use wire topiary frames (available at most garden centres) to train ivy or other climbing plants into interesting shapes. The ivy will take some months to establish a strong outline; in the meantime, miniature white petunias complete the picture.

MATERIALS

45cm (18in) oval terracotta
 windowbox
Crocks (broken pots) or other
 suitable drainage material
Compost (soil mix)
Slow-release plant food granules
Wire topiary frame
Pins made from garden wire
Plant rings

PLANTS

2 variegated ivies
4 miniature white petunias

IVIES

PETUNIA

1 Place a layer of drainage material in the base of the windowbox. Fill the windowbox with compost (soil mix), working in 2 teaspoons of slow-release plant food granules.

2 Plant the two ivies, one in front of the other in the centre of the windowbox.

3 Position the topiary frame in the centre of the windowbox and use pins to hold it in place.

4 Wrap the stems of ivy around the stem of the frame, and then around the frame itself.

5 Cut away any straggly stems and use plant rings to secure the ivy to the frame.

6 Plant the petunias around the topiary ivy. Water thoroughly and stand in light shade.

GARDENER'S TIP

Maintain the shape of the ivy with regular trimming
and training – 5 minutes once a week will create a better shape
than 15 minutes once a month.

PLANT IVY AT ANY TIME OF YEAR,
PETUNIAS IN SPRING

Star-jasmine in a villandry planter

The soft, seductive scent of the star-jasmine makes this a perfect container to place by the side of a door where the scent will be appreciated by all who pass through.

STAR-
JASMINE

MATERIALS

50cm (20in) villandry planter or similar, preferably self-watering
Equal mix loam-based compost (soil mix) and standard compost
Slow-release plant food granules
Bark chippings

PLANTS

Star-jasmine (Trachelospermum jasminoides)

GARDENER'S TIP

Use a plastic liner inside all large planters. It is easier to remove the liner when replanting rather than dismantle the entire container.

PLANT IN LATE SPRING OR EARLY SUMMER

1 Feed the wicks through the holes in the base of the liner.

2 Fill the water reservoir in the base of the planter to the top of the overflow pipe, and place the liner inside the planter.

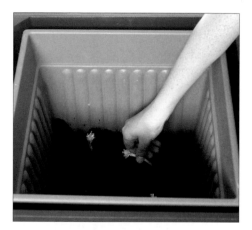

3 Fill the bottom of the liner with compost (soil mix) while pulling through the wicks so that they reach the level of the roots.

4 Remove the jasmine from its pot, gently tease the roots loose and stand it in the planter.

NOTE *Steps 1–3 are for self-watering planters only.*

5 Add compost (soil mix) and firm it around the root-ball of the jasmine. Scatter 2 tablespoons of plant food granules on the surface, and gently work them into the top layer of compost with the trowel.

6 Mulch around the plant with a layer of bark chippings, then water. Check the reservoir of the self-watering container once a week and top up if necessary. Conventional pots should be watered daily in the early morning or evening during hot weather.

A silver and white wall basket

The helichrysum's silvery foliage and cool blue lavender flowers give a delicate colour scheme which would look good against a weathered background.

MATERIALS

30cm (12in) wall basket
Sphagnum moss
Compost (soil mix)
Slow-release plant food granules

PLANTS

2 lavenders (Lavandula dentata *var.* candicans)
Osteospermum *'Whirligig'*
2 Helichrysum petiolare

OSTEOSPERMUM

LAVENDER

HELICHRYSUM

GARDENER'S TIP

The lavender used in this project is fairly unusual – if you wish, you can substitute a low-growing variety such as 'Hidcote'.
Keep the helichrysum in check by pinching out its growing tips fairly regularly or it may take over the basket.

PLANT IN SPRING

1 Line the basket with moss and half-fill it with compost (soil mix).

2 Mix in a half-teaspoon of plant food granules. Plant the lavenders in each corner.

3 Plant the osteospermum in the centre of the basket then add the helichrysums on either side.

4 Angle the plants to encourage them to trail over the side of the basket. Fill with compost (soil mix). Water the basket and hang.

Chinese water garden

In China, glazed pots are frequently used as small ponds in courtyards.
This pot contains a water lily, a flowering rush and an arum lily.

FLOWERING
RUSH

WATER LILY

ARUM LILY

MATERIALS

Water lily basket
Piece of hessian
Aquatic compost (soil mix)
Large bucket
70cm (28in) glazed pot
Putty (optional)
Bricks

PLANTS

Compact water lily
  (Nymphaea tetragona)
Flowering rush
  (Butomus umbellatus)
Arum lily (Zantedeschia
  aethiopica)

1 Line the basket with hessian, insert the water lily and top up with aquatic compost (soil mix). Lower the basket into a bucket of water to settle the compost.

2 If the glazed pot has a drainage hole, plug it with putty and leave to harden overnight. Use bricks to create platforms for the two potted plants.

3 Before filling the pot with water, position the rush so that its pot will be fully submerged and the arum lily so that the pot will be half-submerged.

4 Fill the pot with water and gently lower the water lily into position – its leaves should float on the surface. This water garden will do best in a sunny position.

GARDENER'S TIP

This arrangement is not recommended for anyone with small children; they can drown in a surprisingly small amount of water.

PLANT IN LATE SPRING OR
EARLY SUMMER

A topiary planting

BOX PYRAMID

BOX BALL

BACOPA

Topiary box plants remain in
their pots in this windowbox.
A mulch of bark conceals the
pots and retains moisture, and
small pots of white bacopa add
another dimension to the
sculptured design.

MATERIALS
64cm (25in) terracotta planter
Bark chippings

PLANTS
Box pyramid in 5 litre (9in) pot
2 box balls in 5 litre (9in) pots
5 pots white bacopa

1 Water all the plants
thoroughly. Stand the box
pyramid in its pot in the centre of
the container.

2 Stand the box balls on either
side of the pyramid.

3 Fill the container with bark
chippings to hide the pots.

4 Plunge the pots of bacopa in the bark at the front of the container.
Stand in light shade. Water regularly.

GARDENER'S TIP

Provided the box plants are not root-bound they will be quite happy
in their pots for a year. If the leaves start to lose their glossy
dark green colour, it is a sign that they need a feed. Sprinkle a long-term
plant food on the surface of the pots and boost with a liquid feed.

PLANT BOX AT ANY TIME OF THE YEAR,
AND BACOPA IN SPRING

Index

ACKNOWLEDGEMENTS
All projects were created by
Stephanie Donaldson and
photographed by Marie O'Hara
unless stated below.

Contributors
Clare Bradley: pp 64, 65.
Blaise Cooke: pp 18, 19, 76,
77, 78, 79, 86. Tessa Evelegh:
pp 10t, 12t, 12m, 13, 14.
Peter McHoy: p 12b. Karin
Hossack: pp 31, 32. Liz
Wagstaff: p 29, 30.

Photographers
John Freeman: pp 14m, 14b,
15b, 18, 19, 20, 23r, 33, 40,
41, 59, 64, 65, 76, 77, 78, 79,
86, 90, 91, 93. Don Last: p25r.
Debbie Patterson: pp. 10t, 12t,
12m, 13, 14m, 14b, 15b, 29,
30, 31, 32, 87. Peter McHoy:
pp 24, 25l.